Tender Age

Tender Age

Luiza Flynn-Goodlett

Winner of the Charlotte Mew Prize

HEADMISTRESS PRESS

ISBN 9781733534529

Cover art by Jessica Rankin
Skyweed: 12 July, 2010
2012
Graphite, ink and watercolour on paper
60 x 60 in. (152.4 x 152.4 cm) (unframed)
62 x 62 3/16 x 2 3/8 in. (157.5 x 158 x 6 cm) (framed)
© the artist. Photo © White Cube (Christopher Burke, New York)

Cover & book design by Mary Meriam.

PUBLISHER
Headmistress Press
60 Shipview Lane
Sequim, WA 98382
Telephone: 917-428-8312
Email: headmistresspress@gmail.com
Website: headmistresspress.blogspot.com

To Ana, my first reader.

CONTENTS

CONFESSIONAL

Although grandma made sure I saw the inside

of a church once a year, there's no communion

for the unbaptized, and certainly no sliding into

the lacquered booth to whisper through a screen.

But she can't stop me telling now—how I slipped

the cat's bowl through a crack in the door to avoid

shit-caked fur, eyes yellow with death; shoved my

brother down a slide, broke his arm; never held

infant necks right. So cue absolution, my heavy

plait shorn. A shadow shifts behind the screen—

Is that you, redeemer? Or still me, ear cupped

to my own voice, ready for the good word.

OUTHOUSES

The first accompanies my arrival—

recipient of bucket-borne offerings

from an unplumbed birthing house—

its only window, a crescent moon.

Next is beyond our chicken coop,

spiderwebs in the warm air under

the seat. Many follow—roomy as

coffins, with doors that won't latch

and me, rifling yellowed funny

papers, sounding out sentiments

cut into the walls, as childhood's

endless slide carousel clicks by.

YOU ASK ABOUT DESIRE

Pre-AOL, miles from any neighbors,
with only a flickering black-and-white
TV and stacks of *National Geographic*

to go on, it's no surprise that I thought
myself immune. Sure, I papered walls
with Taylor Hanson's *Teen Beat* glory,

bit lips in slick backseats, but not until
New York, crossing Bowery, did I spot
its first true messenger, in a button-up,

hair high and tight, boots gleaming. She
didn't glance at my dropped jaw, walked
on. It's still that rare—a phosphorescent

flicker in deep-sea dark. Still stops me
short—in our hallway mirror, you lift
ties to the hollow of your throat, decide.

CHILDHOOD FEAR

The story may have been passed over
my head at a party—kindergartner who

took refuge, tragic consequences—but
I don't think so. Still, on nightly loop,

I saw legs swallowed by its dark mouth,
then flash flood, muddy Keds found

weeks later. It makes even less sense
given my fearlessness—cannonballing

off waterfalls, cajoling cousins to build
a raft, travel the river like Huck—yet, at

a storm drain's rusted rim, I dissolved
into trembling. Maybe it was vertigo—

father, a life-long caver, never minded
being submerged, just lifted his chin,

sipped air—and I was obscurely drawn
to this first trapdoor out I'd found.

FAMILY TREE

I come from those who sliced branches off

blighted ones, grafted elsewhere. I too carry

shears, worry the handle. My taproot's rotten

on both sides—one's a scrum of drunks; other,

the owners of slaves, all tallied in documents

donated to the museum. How easy to snip my

name, like a paper doll, from those margins,

shut the cabinet. But when shears slip, open

a flap, that same sap flows, whiskey-red.

I'm made of the damn stuff. See it dribble

out of my mouth, over the vast white page.

DANGERS

Like the girl we see tackled, roll her
a smoke as she rubs the sore shoulder
where her purse was yanked free; or,

out night-jogging, the man who holds
a Bowie knife at his hip and watches

passing women with his whole body;
even the frat boys chucking hatchets
at redwoods beside an intersection

as girlfriends pass a flask. Countless
see the salt circles of others' bodies,

toe them open. Told the creek held
geodes, I went willingly, have tasted
nothing but the salt scattered since.

GHOST STORY

I met one. Not in a traditional
getup of chains—mine walked
through the walls of a young life
like mist, took all he could carry,

vanished. Scrying led to objects—
an embroidered dress, mud-caked
shoelaces, geode—held so long in
wondering hands that all traces of

him rubbed off. And, since he was
spirited away to some other school,
along with any memories of those
woods, face lit from above, might

be anywhere, anyone a few years
older. Sheltered by this question's
hook, I summon him—shade with
hands of sand, my only lonely twin.

WHEN RETURNING SOUTH

Obtain straight planks painted

bone-white. Nail right angles.

Once complete, drag the box

to a cistern or attic where you

won't be disturbed. Then fold

in half and in half again, like

a handkerchief. Yes, it hurts,

the space smaller than it first

appears. Unhitch joints, snap

neck so your chin lolls. Bend

knees as you draw the lid. It's

rough on your cheek, almost

cozy, just how you remember.

IT'S EASIER THESE DAYS

At least, in our apartment.
Outside, maybe not. Seems
men can't stand what won't
come when called, snarl as
pace quickens. Sure, clubs
are no longer raided, red

light urging, *Hurry—switch
partners.* And we *can* make
yearly pilgrimages to towns
that spawned us, avoiding
truck-stop bathrooms along
the way. But it's provisional

grace, mouths *fags* once we
clear the porch. And those
who guilt, *Come home,* never
saw that slip of sand where,
naked despite fog, we swim
under a rusty Golden bow.

ORCHIDS

Three transplanted stems,
stoic in snow. What potent
mix of hope and ignorance

obscured the moss clinging
to their roots, quite unlike
courtyard's mud? Though

I've done much the same—
brandished best intentions
to shield any manner of

mischief. See, no matter
when you read this, a man
has just been shot, holding

a thing nothing like a gun.
Of what use are *intentions*
to him? A better question

is who's allowed to intend,
and who is only an object
of intention. Notice how

I tell it—the orchids' story,
one of mistake, instead of
living things, their deaths.

And how, in both cases,
a quick-falling whiteness
cloaks everything in itself.

SHARD

Hours of salt soaks,
sewing needle held

to lighter, digging
around, and I've got

you. Once peroxide's
poured, you'll rise on

pink foam—a frigate
capsized at sunset, all

souls lost. Ointment
quiets my gasp. But,

like the confetti of
nails on a barn's dirt

floor, you're envoy
of what once ended

us, what won't stop
rapping at the door.

SHELLEY'S HEART

You've heard the story—the body
burns, but his heart, stillborn-blue

under char, won't. Mary shrouds
it in silk to wear as clutch at her

wrist; and, when her turn comes,
leaves it on her desk, wrapped in

his last poem. Grief granted weight
at last, yet still portable—all of us

in line at self-checkout, shackled
by these charm bracelets, some up

to their elbows. Only, which part
to save? Of you, nothing—I'd push

the barrow back out, use what's
left of myself to feed the flames.

CHOOSING A TRANSITIONAL OBJECT

Snip Hansons from *Teen Beat* while debating
Taylor versus Zac so passionately a curl escapes
its barrette and your best friend tucks it behind

an ear before it catches on lip-gloss. Start a fight
so she'll get picked up early, forgetting a lanyard
on the den's yellow shag. Wander past beehives,

quiet for winter, into the pasture where a hayloft
gasps open. Bite nails bloody telling yourself how
stupid she is, the fence posts kicked for emphasis.

Eat slices of bread from the bag. Then, diary
on knee, scribble page after page of *not a lesbian*
before securing the lock, removing its toy key.

PRETTY

Pity those who cupped its flame
through adolescence's long windy
season—bent over compacts, lips

glitter-gloss gritty, long hair parted
in the middle—their unsteady gait,
bodies balanced like waiters' trays

of wine. Later, we'd learn the trick's
to fix eyes like a dancer, forget. No
one knew how then, so flickered at

each school-day gust, dripped wax,
while my wet wick wouldn't catch, no
matter the match. Dumb putty body,

sweet as our half-blind tabby, little
did I know of the molten fire at your
core, volcanic but for my readiness.

THE LIPSTICK LOUNGE

One summer, there's an oxygen bar
upstairs, another, skinheads behind
the dumpster. Always, pool tables,
dartboard felt giving way. Karaoke's

Friday, mulleted owner sidling out
from behind the bar, mic in hand.
Light up anywhere; that law hasn't
reached us. But cabs don't stop, so

you'll want to hitch in a stranger's
truck, bum endless smokes. Maybe
you were born here too, beneath
a sticky banquette, took first steps

to a quavering rendition of *Galileo,*
and are still tethered—heart, that
stall with the bum lock, opens at
a nudge, pays for the next round.

IN SECURITY

Flush with fever, we tug off
boots, unwind scarves, shuck
laptops into bins. Have you

escaped secondary screening?
Never in this city, drawl thick
as you're taken aside. There's

customary confusion over who
ought to perform the pat down
as I hover beside the same palms

I stood by when they confiscated
a birdcage, sure its head-scarved
owner stashed explosives under

shredded paper. Her canary got
out, of course, battered endless
windows above a people mover.

When our flight boarded, we left
her posed as Saint Francis—nuts
proffered, lips pursed to whistle.

This time, you're the faint flutter.
And I step into her shadow, open
ribcage to an improbable return.

EVIDENCE LOCKER

Mother's downsizing,

hands over a shoebox
of snapshots labeled in

a loopy childish hand.

I stash it in the closet
until bored, still don't

expect my crime-scene-

red dress, menagerie
along the collar. I'm

barefoot at creek-edge,

squinting into the sun.
It hadn't happened yet—

proof's in how my face

opens, wobbly as unset
yolk, to whoever holds

the camera. So, shred

or kiss it? No, ball it
up and swallow, make

her part of me again.

OUR PARENTS' DEATH

Spoken of almost without
a tremor, it takes shape as

a cargo-laden ship, smudge
listing on the horizon. Too

soon, we know, it will dock,
freight fill rooms, seawater

overflow pockets. But that's
a ways off. For now, we're

on the pier, feeding quarters
into a viewer, can just make

out a massive hull, tugboats
alongside, before we're sun-

dizzy, so step aside to let
the next in line have a try.

LAST WISHES

He taps a gold-capped molar,
Have the undertaker pull these

before they put me in the ground.
Don't let 'em tell you otherwise.

Won't forget, I assure, picturing
elderly southern ladies in hats

and gloves bent over the casket
while mid-century dental work

clacks around the bottom of
my purse. Doubt they'll allow

it; and, anyway, the youngest
already claimed the lot to melt

into a ring. Fine by me, since
I'd prefer them whole—dice

polished each morning, and
against odds, cast with our lot.

MY FATHER'S DAUGHTER

We're a pair of flat feet, cleft

palate's grin, deer skulls boiled

to keep. Catfish, we whisker

what squirms at the lake's silt

heart, army-crawl down shafts

carved by runoff, lift loafers to

examine a crushed spider, only

pray for more of the same. Look—

on a trail clear up the hillside,

a father rests a toddler on his

shoulders, hands her scraps of

beauty, speaks its many names.

CHILDLESS

It's almost too late, but maybe
we're wrong to wall ourselves

on the side with crisp sheets,
pour-overs, mornings rifling

the paper. We visit the other—
shoulders are spit up on; dogs

track mud, drop wet tennis
balls at feet—ward off chaos

with a Tide pen, sigh once in
the car. At home, everything's

in place—after cleaners come,
it takes a minute to return

order, right magnets dusted
crooked. No surprises await—

chickenpox, rescued robin's
eggs warming under a lamp—

in their place, a perishable
buffet, shortcut to the exit.

LAST GASP

That's how these years will seem—a breath

above the current, long enough to glimpse

a conifer-lined shore, swim in that direction.

But here, in it, respite is endless as a summer

afternoon, wasps troubling the pitcher of tea,

and having come, dented, through hailstorms,

we settle in. But such fevers break. So I slip

into past tense, hold sweetness in my cheek

like hard candy I can't bear to finish. And

what did you say while kneading dough,

chin flour-white? *Most aren't even given this.*

CAREWORN

The fallacy must have been

cultivated during decades

of dorm rooms, apartments

where bricks molted mold,

bare minimum was boxed

to keep—I'm perplexed by

how silver tarnishes, paint

scrubs off ladles, rags get

dingier. What a shock to

inhabit what I'd only sped

past, viewed from a train—

green smears, blue stripe

of river. And hard to trust

what holds still—hangs

frames, fills rooms with

animal smell, breathes

into my hair all night.

HIGHWAY 1

In the eastern shoulder's
scrub and hunched trees,

a doe noses the air, flicks
ears toward car's rumble.

Headlights swim over two
fauns, frozen beside her.

We all hang there a long
moment—her knee lifted

to bolt and your hands
that still smell of my salt,

gripping the wheel—then
round a bend, and this

junker—now, ark—ferries
us into the rest of our lives.

ABOUT THE AUTHOR

Luiza Flynn-Goodlett is the author of the forthcoming collection *Look Alive*, winner of the 2019 Cowles Poetry Book Prize from Southeast Missouri State University Press, along with six chapbooks, most recently *Shadow Box*, winner of the 2019 Madhouse Press Editor's Prize. Her poetry can be found in *Third Coast, Pleiades, The Journal, The Common*, and elsewhere. She serves as editor-in-chief of *Foglifter* and lives in sunny Oakland, California.

ACKNOWLEDGMENTS

Many thanks to the editors of the following publications, in which these poems appeared, sometimes in earlier versions:

Barrow Street: "Last Gasp"

The Common: "Choosing a Transitional Object"

Gertrude: "The Lipstick Lounge"

The Journal: "Careworn"

the minnesota review: "Orchids"

The Shallow Ends: "Highway 1"

Pleiades: "Confessional, Family Tree"

HEADMISTRESS PRESS BOOKS

Spine - Sarah Caulfield

I Wore the Only Garden I've Ever Grown - Kathryn Leland

Diatribe from the Library - Farrell Greenwald Brenner

Blind Girl Grunt - Constance Merritt

Acid and Tender - Jen Rouse

Beautiful Machinery - Wendy DeGroat

Odd Mercy - Gail Thomas

The Great Scissor Hunt - Jessica K. Hylton

A Bracelet of Honeybees - Lynn Strongin

Whirlwind @ Lesbos - Risa Denenberg

The Body's Alphabet - Ann Tweedy

First name Barbie last name Doll - Maureen Bocka

Heaven to Me - Abe Louise Young

Sticky - Carter Steinmann

Tiger Laughs When You Push - Ruth Lehrer

Night Ringing - Laura Foley

Paper Cranes - Dinah Dietrich

On Loving a Saudi Girl - Carina Yun

The Burn Poems - Lynn Strongin

I Carry My Mother - Lesléa Newman

Distant Music - Joan Annsfire

The Awful Suicidal Swans - Flower Conroy

Joy Street - Laura Foley

Chiaroscuro Kisses - G.L. Morrison

The Lillian Trilogy - Mary Meriam

Lady of the Moon - Amy Lowell, Lillian Faderman, Mary Meriam

Irresistible Sonnets - ed. Mary Meriam

Lavender Review - ed. Mary Meriam

www.ingramcontent.com/pod-product-compliance
Lightning Source LLC
Chambersburg PA
CBHW072020060426
42446CB00044B/3196